Is There Life

Is There Life

Bedell Phillips

Cover photograph
from NASA Ames Research Center

Printed in the United States of America

ISBN: 978-1-950381-84-5

Library of Congress Control Number 2021943921

Published by Piscataqua Press
32 Daniel St., Portsmouth, NH 03801

Printed using the Garamond font

Dedication

For Jason, Celeste, Nina, Johnny, Eliot, Torrey, Alice, and Summer
because they bring me joy

Poet's Notes

Invention of 'Thrums' as a poetic form has driven Bedell's work
in the last several years. Thrums are those threads left on the loom
once a tapestry is removed. They are the poem's last line: the zap,
crux, or its essence. Although Bedell often writes in the thrum format,
she occasionally uses traditional when the poem requires.

Contents

Morning Advent

mackerel sky
early daybreak moon rising
one gull floats

gift of hope

Phenomenon

the oxbow curved to the west
dazzling sun on blazing water

in front of its curve
a wide stripe of sparkling light

then the water current
ordinary movement ordinary color

then another blazing stripe like
fake diamonds on a gown

at the river's end
a solid light band

like a silver ingot

Gumbo Limbo Nesting

rosy rust bark on thick round trunk
joining flat lateral branches
makes a soft curved crotch perch

from the earth they fly to a tree
appearing brownish but with a white
behind that shows both in motion and at rest

the female northern flicker finds her safe nest
nearby sits the colorful male singing
cheep cheep cheep

Great Blue Heron

great blue walked with purpose
onto the golf course
halted for a full two minutes

next went along the lake's edge
with care studied the fountain
looked to the sky

then fully extended
eyed the water's ripples

walked right in and found dinner

Cold Day

the field was turning brown
sheeps' breath rose in clear air
cheviots bundled together

pressing their bodies against one another
thick soft fur clustered
ears laid onto each other

the overlap insulating against the freeze

Success

small New England village
old houses big yards
spotted dogs
searching for their spot

Journey

three Canadian geese
at the pond's edge

finish snacking waded in
following the leader

into the lily pads
disturbing the flowers

two more followed
all the way to the end

Cormorant in the Central Current

water going from Stratham to Portsmouth
filled with yesterday's rain
as in the days of old with the gundalow

dark head matched the river
he was going nowhere
pushed backwards three times

could not move forward
could not fish
dove to the muddy bottom

out-smarted the current

Escape Christo and the Eyes of God

palm fronds lit from below
long sumptuous strings of lights
high in the sky
lighting grassy sward

Christo artist project
saffron-colored gates
give citizens release
throughout New York's
Central Park

Sierra Madre people
look above to God for
protection using
their God's eye shield

all cleansed: backyard folks, famous radical artist, indigenous tribes

Pebbles
for Jane Hirshfield

In the Barn

goats always butt
even little children

Tests
returned cancer results cumulonimbus sky
with a thin sweet after glow edging the earth

resurrection gleam

Brocade of the Sea

perch prefer to feed on the edge of the inlet
whales like the deep center waters

Disaster Recovery

Stavanger langoustinos
from Norway then
herring tartare with herbed celery
listening to Grieg
eating grapes in the dark

find comfort where you can

Jupiter Tailor

a small mini mall shop
basket weave inlaid floor

20 commercial sewing machines
mint colored walls with bracket

holding single shelf throughout
the long room loaded with colored spools

twelve jeweled wedding gowns
cavernous closet with completed dresses

mannequin 1974
stenciled on the linen fabric

two metal dials to adjust
bust and hip size

sicilian Sophia Loren face
greets me smiling proud

Return to Paradise

the same apartment
same stunning palm trees
same lavish inlet

but the water was not on
a friend came pulled the lever
but then no hot water

she found the complex manager
nearby in the shed he came in
found the switch

so much trouble for just basic needs

Okavango Delta

Hippos flourish in the Okavango Delta. In the smaller pools
they attract fish and pelicans in the thousands. Feeding on
the grassy matter they clean out the pool in just a few days.
For safety, fish gather around the hippos. Pods of pelicans have a
feeding frenzy, making the hippos irritable and stressed. Opening their
gigantic mouths showing their tusks. Crocodiles eat the casualties.

Hippos must live in water. But fires sweep across the delta floodplain,
consuming their grass. The dominant male searches for more water,
while the other males fight for dominance. Smokey aftermath creates
dust swirls on their paths, no longer enough water to cover their bodies.
Desperate they develop the ability to ruminate, regurgitating grass
from their stomachs.

Delta fingers reach into the desert. Hippos treck across their paths onto
the dusty land. Their thick hide protects them from the sun, but their
underbelly must remain moist. Their pools continue to get crowded.
More different animals arrive. Lions stake them out. The hippos are
dying of thirst but stand firm even though the lions are now close,
fighting to get their share of water.

During these challenges, a flood creeps down the delta.
Relief is coming. The water rushes closer along the hippo paths
previously dried out. Delta water has flowed once again in the channels.
Returning life to the hippos and their delta habitat.
All that was once lost is now regained.

Cartier

They were millennials. Her boyfriend thought she was super hot. He bought her an expensive classic watch. Went into Cartier and was wowed by their sales people dressed in white tie formal wear. They were to go away with his friend, the son of Luigi, who owned Ferrari in New York. They raced him from Manhattan to Connecticut.

All in bathing suits, she wore her new bikini. They drank Cosmos. It was really hot. Luigi bellowed, "Wanna play Marco Polo?" Instantly, they all lept into the pool. She rose up screaming, "My watch, my watch."

Luigi said, "No problem, I do that all the time." They all went in the house. He said, "Just put it in the oven." The couple was shocked. "Come on, don't be assholes. Put it at 200 degrees. It'll be fine."

Back in New York she walked into Cartier. Claude came up to her smiling. She giggled, "You're looking good, I've always liked those long black coats." "May I help you, perhaps something new, perhaps earrings?"

"Nope, I am actually here with a problem, my watch." "Delighted, Madame, may I take a look at it?" He was gone quite a while, which was just fine. She looked at the diamonds.

He returned. "Upon examination, I am wondering." She looked blankly at him. Claude stated, "I don't understand. Can you tell me what was happening when the watch stopped?"

Humiliated and mortified, she managed, "Huh?" Placing the watch on the velvet jeweler's display cloth, he said, "Your gears appeared to have melted."

She looked at his clear blue eyes, had no answer.

Front Yard

small house
tiny lawn
packed full of
strange scarecrows

both with blackened branch arms
pumpkin heads
sitting on a bench

faces grinning in chilling light

Scarecrow

Uncle Sam in formal clothes
his wife with long colonial dress
high laced neck

time warp sentinels

Skeletons

dense evergreen arborvitae
edge the country road
thick green-covered twigs
from their darkness peeks a skeleton

A Hanging

full grown macintosh tree
newly fruited
red apples among dying leaves

a skeleton hung by his neck

Spooks

four witches
heads in black toile
covered sports ball

fabric over stick arms
all hands around

touching each other
all the way to the ground

double double toil and trouble
dance of the macabre

Election Year

stout 4 by 4 posts
hurricane proof
mailbox held with
wrought iron
bracket

black veiled witch
spread over the box
interfering with the ballot

Million Dollar Ocean View

a grand L'Orangerie
just like at Versailles
arches facing the water
pillars mark the entrance

each topped with a petite pumpkin

Humble Touch

a mile of grand mansions one with
Georgian arched windows
overlooking the Atlantic

half moon torches the waves crashing the breaker
mansion outlined by granite rock wall
topped by ashlar blocks

one-story high stone columns
crowned with beveled glass lanterns
gleaming through the night

sixteen minute pumpkins embellish each side of the gate

A Bad Seed

The family carved five pumpkins
with special tools from Shaw's
Each kid scooped out the seeds
along with the goop

The oldest boy grabbed a tool
and smashed the seeds
"Don't do that what are you thinking?"
shrieked his mother

Everyone drew a picture onto
their pumpkin's face
The tiny daughter worked slowly
They all brought their masterpieces out front

Except she had trouble with the knives
Her dad explained that
she must make a sawing motion
When she finally finished

all four stairs had a pumpkin
She put hers on the front porch
The teenage neighbor
stared at them as he drove up his drive

Later in the night he came by
swooped up all the pumpkins
smashing them on the road
but forgot the smallest

Obliteration was fun

Tuckertown Road

all the boys loved it but their dad
loved that jeep more than anything
the oldest stole into the back field
driving it grinding the clutch
his father ran outside howling
"stop that stop that"

the next morning their friend Andy came over
all of them got into it
they snuck across to the road
once on the dirt the oldest shouted
"now?"
"nope wait a minute"
"here's a good tree"

at that moment they all opened their doors
smashing the sacred jeep against the tree trunks
screams of glee hooting as loud as a teen can

they loved unbridled destruction

Encounter

that sweet cheese steak smell
in South Philly
she turned around
he was next in line
tall needing a shave
thin hair and a long ponytail
de rigeur in the sixties
still sported it proudly
Camels folded into his T-shirt
the sky was striped
with long swirls and fish scales
she had met him in class
he was wearing Paul Stuart
tweed with soft denim shirt

he had sweet serendipity with NY smarts

iPhone

hot summer day
the poet looked out
on her smoldering water

another death poem
dear Lord
she couldn't fathom

where the words were in the midst
of intellectual casting about
an interruptive Apple ding

"hey babe how ya doin' "

Saw Many Basements

he was the middle brother
so cute handsome redhead

a fuck-around in the middle school
with girls whose mothers worked

made it through law school
hired by Morgan Lewis and Bockius

beloved sister started to age
making her will she thought of him
tromping through the woods together

chosen to pull the plug

On the Beach

stunner female bulbous top
tight bottom

he super fit
perfect abs erect nipples

two chaises
touching on the beach

she asleep with her arms over her head
he sweeps over licks the edge of her armpit

Pool View

freckled legged woman
modest suit black background
large white flowers with wide white straps

next to her tan man bushy mustache
grey hair using his ipad
navy trunks spread eagled

flopped to the side the tip of his penis

The Stranger

In a line in July waiting for admission to a historic building,
a couple waited. The John Paul Jones House was stately
painted yellow with white, small paned windows. He stood
6 foot 2, had blue eyes. She, a blonde, was next to him. They had
gone on 4 dates. Slept together for the first time this morning. A
muscled guy in tight blue active wear came up behind her.
Squeezed her waist. She turned, he gave her the look. Her foolish
boyfriend chatted him up. After awhile the stranger asked, "You
guys want to go for a drink?" Turns out, later they became an item.

A Jainism Temple

The essence of Jainism is to achieve ultimate liberation,
so the immortal soul will live in bliss forever. The supreme
concept is non-violence for every being in the universe,
and its complete health. These temples in India are surrounded
by paved stone and sometimes a colossal pool.

One is next to a Tuberculosis Hospital. TB in India causes
approximately 220,000 deaths per year. The World Heath Organization
reports the TB death rate in India is 38.5%. The disease is highly
contagious.

Before entering the monumental domed temple, the masses place their
hands in the immense reflecting pool. All have living souls and must be fed.
They walk the pillared portico first, move by the small room for the cult
images and pass through the soaring sanctuary. Next a series of monks,
who feed all that come, scoop from huge bowls with their hands.

Jewish Experience

on a street in Queens New York
she was going to marry a Jewish guy
she liked him and
his family was fabulous

the synagogue was magnificent
spacious and airy with huge
stained glass behind the Torah

after the ceremony
they all congregated out front she and her dad
had to go back to New Hampshire
she knew she'd miss him

the road was loaded with people speaking fast spanish
she and her dad searched for their car
the hunt was unnerving
at last they found it her dad got in and said

"They all wear those stupid hats"

Diversity in Maimonides Medical Center

A thirty year old Irish Catholic nurse in Borough Park, Brooklyn treated a Hasidic in his mid-forties with chest pain. He was successfully released and went home to his family.

Traditionally, in the Intensive Care Unit, the front desk had holiday decorations: Jewish, Catholic, and Asian. He returned. In gratitude, exclaimed, "You saved my life!" Stood as tall as he could, and presented his nurse with two statues. One of a sainted Catholic priest, the other, a Rabbi. She was so honored, she went immediately to the nursing station and placed them exactly in the middle of the decorations.

Harsh-faced, bald, and angry, the hospital administrator ordered, "Get those outta here." Refusing his authority, after work she went to Steinbergs on 47th Street. Brought back to her ward silver festoons of dreidels and a fake hemlock tree.

Demonstrating everyone's right to religious freedom.

A Civil Rights Martyr

From Keene New Hampshire he went south to Selma. Jonathan Daniels was young and white. Committed to equality for all. At first he was turned away from Selma's Brown Chapel. But that did not stop him. He planned and participated in the Selma March. During the march he protected a 17 year old from a bullet. Jonathan was shot and killed on August 19, 1965.

Mockingbird on a Lamppost

babe in the Florida pool cogitating
covid emails for the wrong shot
anguish for her daughter—three weeks with it
agony with foot pain

across the water with white stripes
in her tail she lands singing
hew hew rasps whistling and trills

Covid and the Sandwich

things were not good at work
his boss got covid
just when the competition got fierce
had to go to the river

he'd found his favorite village shop
got a lavish croissant with
melted manchego and mortadella ham

it was warm in his hand
wrapped in tinfoil
marked with thick red magic marker

made no sense
a big letter M for meat?
turned the other way a W

his engine was off
the sandwich top notch
and even better the melted cheese
which he licked off the wrapper's deep crevices

sated clutch down shoved the gear shift
hit the gas the car wouldn't move
looked up there were a bunch of rocks

between him and the water
why am I not moving
my car is fucked up

stymied hands in the air "what is
going on" he smashes the dash and his elbow
spills his coffee

oh I've got it I gotta turn the car on

This Actually Happened

A Chinese doctor, Li Wenliang, who tried to issue the first warning about the deadly Coronavirus outbreak, has died at Wuhan Central Hospital, the hospital reported. He had been hospitalized for at least three weeks having contracted the virus while working there.

On December 30, 2019 after noticing seven cases of a virus that he thought looked like SARS, the doctor had sent out a Weibo chat-group warning to fellow medics to wear protective clothing to avoid infection. The cases were thought to come from the Huanan Seafood market in Wuhan and the patients were in quarantine in his Institute.

The doctor's post read "Hello everyone, This is Li Wenliang, an ophthalmologist at Wuhan Central Hospital." Three days later police paid him a visit and told him to stop "making false comments." He returned to work and caught the virus from a patient. In a later post he described how on January 10th he started coughing, the next day he had a fever and two days later he was in hospital. He was diagnosed with the Coronavirus on January 30, 2020.

Dr. Li Wenliang was hailed as a hero for raising the alarm about the Coronavirus in the early days of the outbreak. There had been contradictory reports about his death, but the People's Daily announced he died at 02:58 on Friday, February 7, 2020 (18:58 GMT Thursday). His death was confirmed by the Wuhan hospital where he worked and was being treated.

Reported by: BBC News China February 7, 2020

This Never Happened

Dear President of the People's Republic of China Xi Jinping,

From the United States, we send our deep condolences upon the death of Dr. Li Wenliang. We are grieved by the lost of this excellent man and his fine research on the matter of the Coronavirus.

I will form a committee of the most gifted American physicians and researchers. To create the most thorough documentation of his work, we would be grateful if you would send a complete copy of his data. We will name this institute the Dr. Li Wenliang Institue for Coronavirus Research.

Yours truly,

Donald J. Trump

A Voyage

phone calls for 3 weeks 6:15 every morning
at last got one, an appointment had to drive
to Miami turned off the highway
into urban blight small low abutting buildings
careful drawings looked like Disney cartoons small lady
with auburn hair red bow pushing empty laundry cart

address that was given blocked by cop cars
told to go to NW12th and NW 7th
with endless line of other cars drove
3 times around the Marlin's baseball stadium
in the car with 3 women over 65
waiting, waiting to move, finally around a corner
guided by endless orange cones one pulled
out her phone scanned match.com for a boyfriend

dark dhuku covered the nurse's head
garbed in sterile drapes approached
with an ipad "show me the icon on your form"
another nurse emerged from the plastic tent carrying
antiseptic blue vial with a long needle
each woman put her arm out the car window
after the vaccine they're told to press
on the blue band aid "how do we get our next shot?"

"just call us"

Trouble

can't sleep
can eat, but it makes you fat
new fridge leaks water
the guarantee 2 days old
pain in the back and feet
and in my heart
lost love, lost health
lost keys

Does He Dare Leave His Car?

5 lanes cement median barrier
huge white truck accelerates
missing his car by 5 inches

slammed on his brakes squeaked
over to the tiny exit opening
just past the airport

painted over the door on cement blocks
SAFELY TRANSPORT AUTO
cars blocking an open door

he climbs around sees inside
25 foot long Trump flag
plywood wooden slab

meets the wall at a diagonal angle
3 keys sit on a plastic plate
"What the fuck is that?"

the place is empty "paid 36K
can't leave my car or the keys here"

Love Moments

Sated baby full of milk
asleep nestled on her shoulder
Grandmother called the long
awaited child "Brother"
After the trial they drove back to NH
took out the cold stuffed turkey
Sat crossed-legged on the living room floor

eating off the carcass with their hands

Relief

she let him drive her car
he totaled it

at home with no car
she turned on Music Choice

that son of a bitch
she had just spent $1,000 on tires

opened the fridge found Saffron Road
Pad Thai with rice noodles

it called for a four minute microwave she added a can of
Margaret Holmes squash with vidalia onions

brought back the sweet comfort of her mother's kitchen

Yin Yang

like the melt of dark dirty snow
cumulonimbus clouds and detritus

clear was covered will blue return
not now
when

Boats Left Hope

So many gone handsome dad
endless mother, brave Nana smart
Grampy

cancer, choked kidney, sneaky
cardiac failure, arteriosclerosis,
stroke, mental illness

the boats have left but I can see the end of the channel

Constellation

mars in the sky
north of the moon
planet of heat and fire

roman god
protector of the empire
blood of battle

violence and conflict
noise and slaughter
red in the night

Is There Life?

Humankind holds endless passion about Mars and its mysteries. Scientists have determined that three billion years ago Mars had a different exterior. A vast ocean covered the northern two thirds of the planet. Astrobiologists have reported this means once: clouds, salty seas, and snow capped peaks existed there similar to on earth. Something made the planet lose all surface water.

The discovery of long rivulet-like streaks on a north and west facing crater rim demonstrate a water process. Research indicates presence of briny molecular water, trapped inside salt crystals which create the visible gully-like features. These rivulets in some places run hundreds of meters.

"However it is too early to assess the implications for life on Mars," according to Mary Beth Wilhelm of NASA's Ames Research Center.

Scientists wonder if the briny water comes from the atmosphere or the ground, stating, "Where the water comes from is still a mystery."

Will we ever know?

Acknowledgements

All gratitude to the literary journals publishing my poems. The author gratefully acknowledges the *Best of the Net*'s nomination for "Thinking about the Violence." Chard deNiord, Tom Sleigh, and Rodney Jones are some but not all of the gifted and patient poets who have guided my work. Deep thanks to my interns, my readers, and my mentor, Tom Lux.

Also by Bedell Phillips

POETRY

Edges of Waves
Thrums & Tapestry
Wolf Tail Glimmer
Where They Land

PROSE

Around the Bend

www.ingramcontent.com/pod-product-compliance
Lightning Source LLC
Chambersburg PA
CBHW022346040426
42449CB00006B/743